COW TO CONE

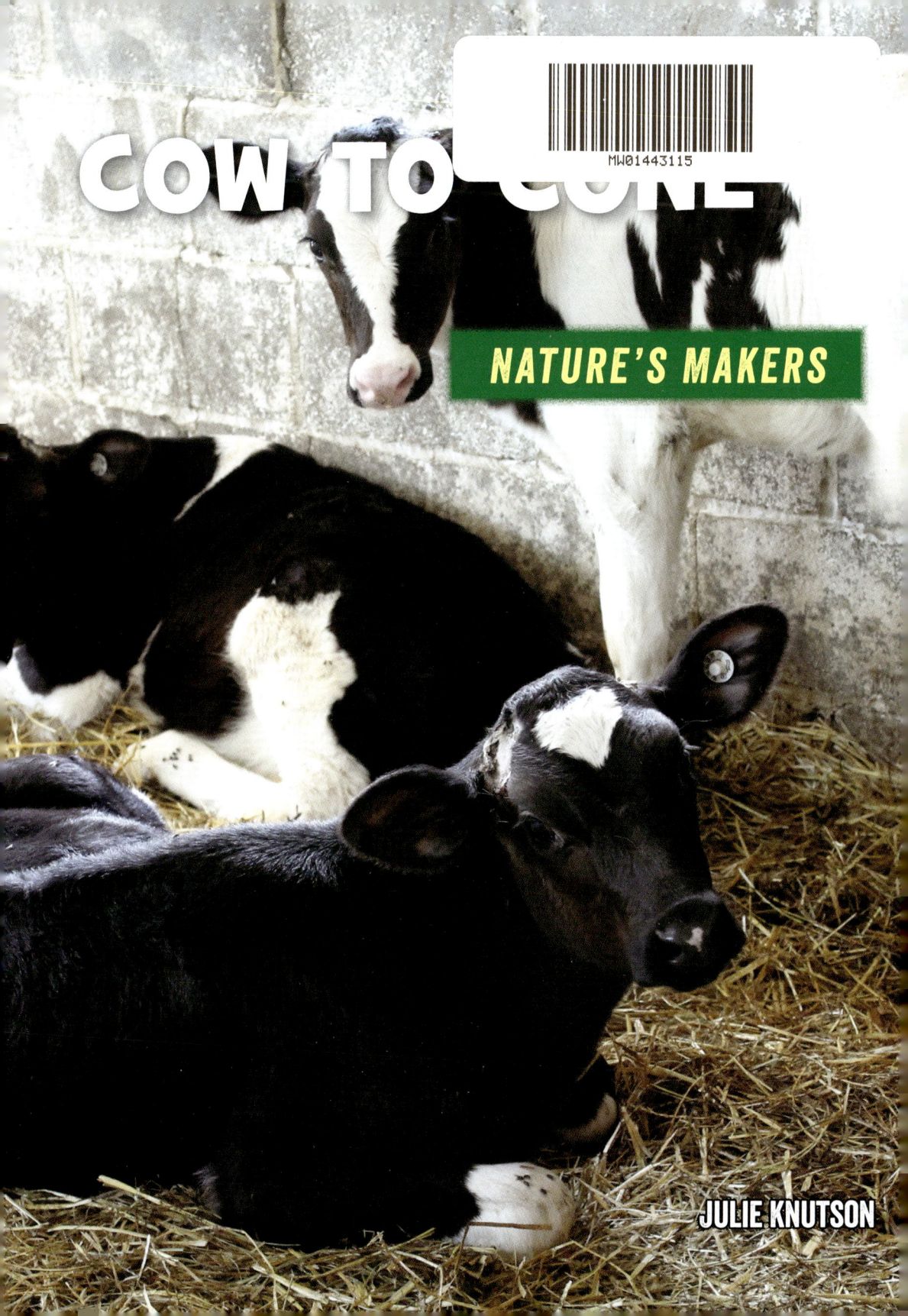

NATURE'S MAKERS

JULIE KNUTSON

Published in the United States of America by Cherry Lake Publishing
Ann Arbor, Michigan
www.cherrylakepublishing.com

Content Advisors: Carolyn Matthews Eaglehouse, owner, Milky Way Farm/Chester Springs Creamery

Photo Credits: © Steve Rudick, cover, 1, 11, 12, 14, 19, 20, 22, 24, 27, 28; © Greg Georgis, 5; © Temple University Libraries, SCRC, Philadelphia, PA, 6; © Courtesy of Chester Springs Creamery/Milky Way Farm, 8, 16

Copyright ©2019 by Cherry Lake Publishing
All rights reserved. No part of this book may be reproduced or utilized in any form or by any means without written permission from the publisher.

Library of Congress Cataloging-in-Publication Data
Names: Knutson, Julie, author. | Knutson, Julie.
Title: Cow to cone / by Julie Knutson.
Description: Ann Arbor : Cherry Lake Publishing, 2019. | Series: Nature's makers | Includes bibliographical references and index.
Identifiers: LCCN 2018036613| ISBN 9781534143005 (hardcover) | ISBN 9781534140769 (pdf) | ISBN 9781534139565 (pbk.) | ISBN 9781534141964 (hosted ebook)
Subjects: LCSH: Ice cream, ices, etc.—Juvenile literature. | Dairy products industry—Juvenile literature. | Farms, Small—Juvenile literature.
Classification: LCC TX795 .K58 2019 | DDC 641.8/62—dc23
LC record available at https://lccn.loc.gov/2018036613

Cherry Lake Publishing would like to acknowledge the work of The Partnership for 21st Century Learning. Please visit www.p21.org for more information.

Printed in the United States of America
Corporate Graphics

ABOUT THE AUTHOR

Julie Knutson is a former teacher who writes from her home in northern Illinois. Researching these books involved sampling a range of farm products, from local honey to heirloom grains to…farm-fresh ice cream! She's thankful to all those who accompanied her on these culinary excursions—most notably to the young ones: Theo, Will, Alex, Ruby, and Olivia.

TABLE OF CONTENTS

CHAPTER 1
The Path from Cow to Cone... 4

CHAPTER 2
The Road to a Creamery 10

CHAPTER 3
What It Takes 18

CHAPTER 4
Meeting Customer Needs 26

READ, RESEARCH, WRITE.. 30
GLOSSARY 31
FURTHER READING 32
INDEX 32

CHAPTER 1

The Path from Cow to Cone

Ice cream shops—they're as unique as the flavors they serve!

Some, like Peddler's Creamery in Los Angeles, California, provide unusual experiences. Here, customers churn their own frozen treats by pedaling a stationary bike. Others, like the Union Dairy in Freeport, Illinois, offer wildly delicious delights. Their house specialty? The Original Holy Cow: a 12-scoop sundae with every topping on the menu!

At Chester Springs Creamery in Pennsylvania, you can get really, *really* close to the source of the ice cream you're eating. In fact, you can enjoy a cone while visiting the very cows

The Original Holy Cow Sundae at the Union Dairy in Freeport, IL, features a dozen scoops of ice cream.

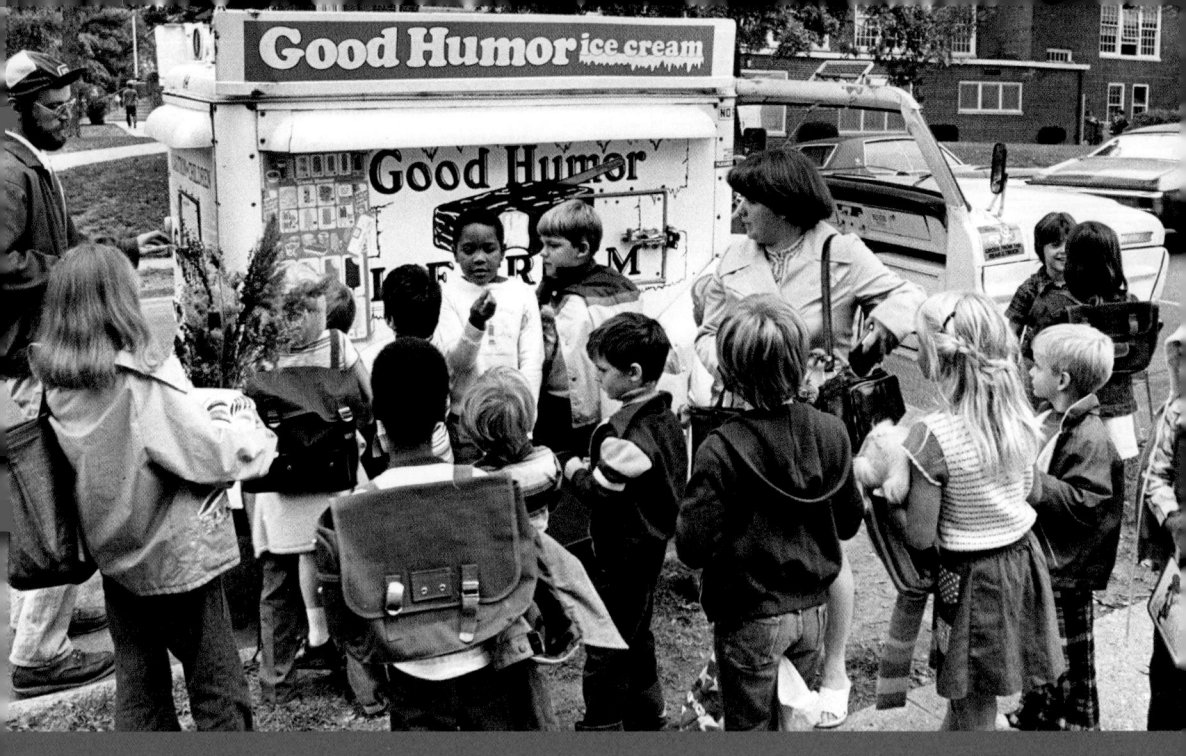

Ice cream trucks have long been a welcome sight for children and adults alike!

whose milk was used to make it. That's because the creamery is located on Milky Way Farm.

Ice cream has a long and global history. It was enjoyed in China as a mix of frozen milk and rice as long ago as 200 BCE. Ancient Greeks and Romans ate snow mixed with honey and fruit. The explorer Marco Polo traveled the Silk Road in the 1300s and brought new ice cream recipes from Asia to Europe.

With the invention of refrigeration and home freezers in the 20th century, ice cream's popularity soared. Companies manufactured it. Customers lined up for it. Whether served in cones or cups, sodas or shakes, at parlors or at home, ice cream was a hit!

Invention of the Cone

Have you ever heard the saying "Necessity is the mother of invention"? Nowhere is this phrase better illustrated than in the creation of the pointy-bottomed ice cream cone.

Two sellers stood side by side at the 1904 World's Fair in St. Louis, Missouri. One, Arnold Fomachou, sold ice cream served in paper cups. The other, Ernest Hamwi, sold Syrian zalibia, or waffles. When Arnold ran out of cups, Ernest made an edible one by forming the waffle into a cone.

The ice cream cone as we know it was born!

[Nature's Makers]

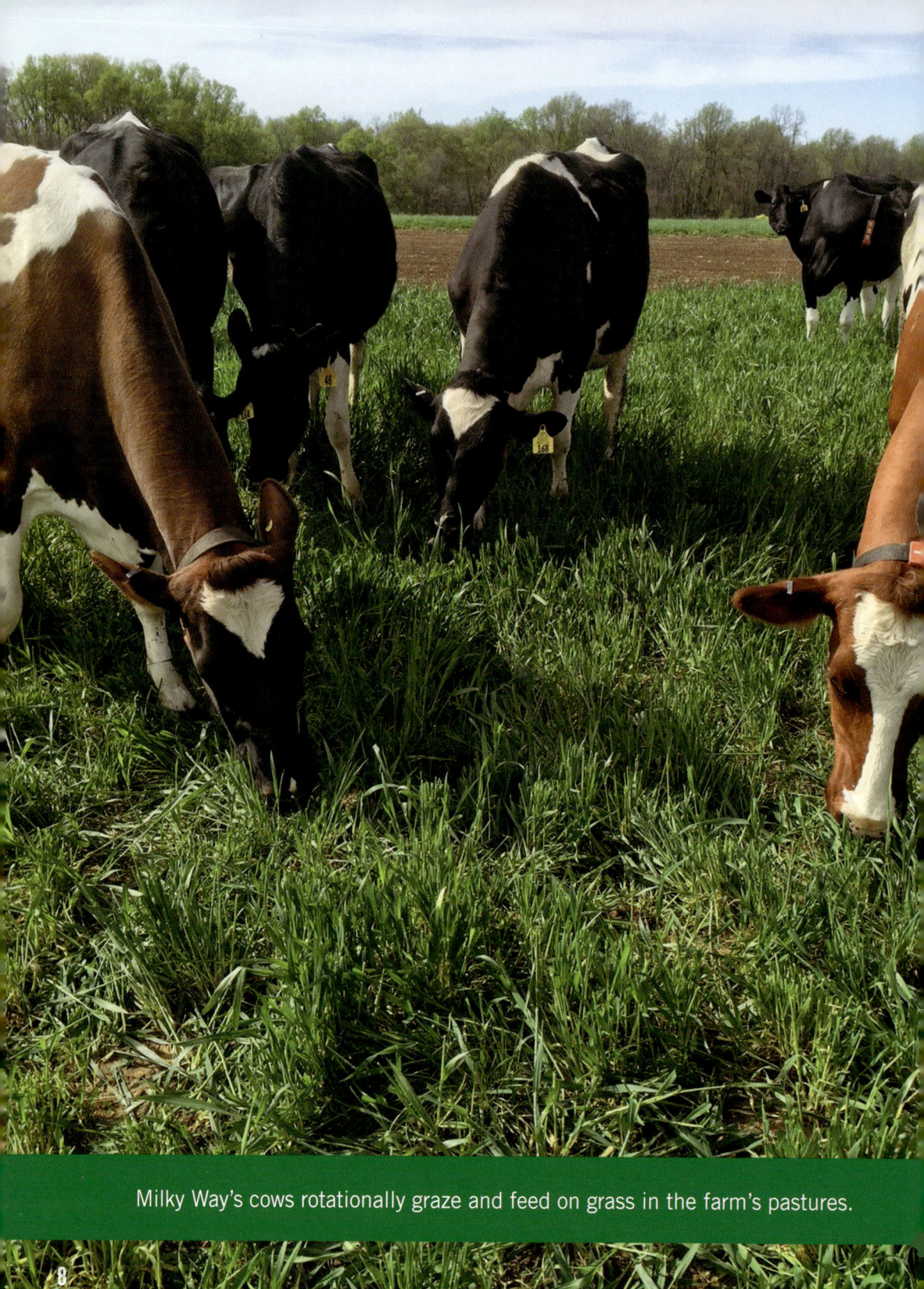

Milky Way's cows rotationally graze and feed on grass in the farm's pastures.

Ice cream relies on a key ingredient: milk. Whether from a cow, goat, or sheep, milk gives ice cream its creamy texture.

The ice cream at Chester Springs Creamery is made with milk from Milky Way Farm's cows. The Matthews family oversees the making of their ice cream. They produce, package, and **distribute** it. This arrangement allows for the freshest possible product. It also creates a personal connection between the people who make the ice cream and the people who buy it.

The farm and creamery's team uses its **human capital**—or knowledge and experience—to manage **natural resources**, like the land and the cows that call it home. They also rely on **physical capital**—like buildings and machines—as part of the production process.

The Road to a Creamery

This site has been farmed for hundreds of years. Arrowheads suggest that Native Americans lived on parts of it before European settlement. European colonists built a farmstead here in the 1760s, and it's been a farm ever since.

In 1902, the 103-acre (42-hectare) plot was purchased by the extended Matthews family. For four generations, they've grown crops like hay, oats, and corn. Starting in 1986, they opened the farm to the community, growing gourds for the fall harvest. On chilly October afternoons, children race through the fields looking for their very own giant pumpkin!

This farmstead has been home to several generations of the Matthews family.

The Creamery, seen here in the background, was built in the early 2000s to serve farm-fresh ice cream to Milky Way's visitors.

Of course, throughout its century-long history, the family has also raised **livestock**, including dairy cows—the stars of this story.

Until 2001, the Matthews' dairy was a strictly **wholesale** operation. This means they sold their herd's milk to larger **cooperatives**. Those groups processed, packaged, and distributed it as milk, cheese, and butter.

But the farm and the world beyond it were changing. Milk prices kept declining. The farm became protected under a state **preservation** program. The Matthews voiced a new commitment to farm education, and people wanted to visit the farm beyond the month of October. As a final factor, a favorite local ice cream parlor closed, creating a market opening.

These circumstances led the family to **diversify** by adding a **retail** operation. The idea for an on-site creamery that manufactured and served ice cream was born.

Carolyn Matthews Eaglehouse is one of the **entrepreneurs** behind the Creamery. Carolyn grew up on this farm. Today, she and her dad, Sam—with support from spouses, siblings, and children—manage its operations. Other family members sell fruit, vegetables, and eggs produced by local farmers.

What inspired Carolyn and her family to start a creamery? While many factors played a role, it ultimately came down to community. Carolyn explains, "Visitors were always saying, 'We really want to visit your farm more than in just October. We want to be able to come as many times as we want!'"

The farm and creamery are a family-operation, with Carolyn and Sam at the helm.

During the October festivities, the family would sell local ice cream from a nearby dairy. Many customers asked if it was made on the farm. When that local shop closed, the Matthews decided it was time to start making their own ice cream.

In the early 2000s, Carolyn and her husband set off on a month-long road trip to draft a plan for a successful retail business. They sampled ice cream across America. They took notes on what they wanted in their creamery. They studied up on retail operations and built their knowledge of what would work best in their town of Chester Springs.

"Our ice cream business was generated as much by community excitement as our own."

– Carolyn Matthews Eaglehouse

The farm is busy in the fall for pumpkin season.

A Year on Milky Way Farm

The activities on Milky Way Farm and at the creamery change with the seasons. Here's an overview of what a typical year looks like:

- *April and May:* The creamery opens on weekends. Many school groups also visit the farm. Fieldwork continues.
- *June through August:* Peak ice cream production, with the creamery operating 6 days a week. Summer campers come to the farm to learn and play. Fieldwork continues, and hay and oats are harvested.
- *September through November:* The creamery returns to weekend hours.
- *October:* The farm welcomes visitors for hayrides, pumpkin picking, and other fall festivities.
- *November:* The creamery closes the weekend before Thanksgiving.
- *December through February:* The quietest months on the farm.
- *March through July:* Calving begins in March and continues through the early summer. Fieldwork also starts.

What It Takes

The cows are the central natural resource that the creamery needs to operate. The success of the Matthews' business depends on this herd.

Carolyn explains, "The farm is tied together through the cows. Think of them as the axle on a wheel. While we need the other aspects of the farm—the creamery, the pumpkins, school visits, and summer camps—to make the wheel go around, it all comes down to the cows. They support our businesses because they provide the draw, but the other business provides the revenue to support them."

Calving season generally runs between March and July and marks the peak of milk production.

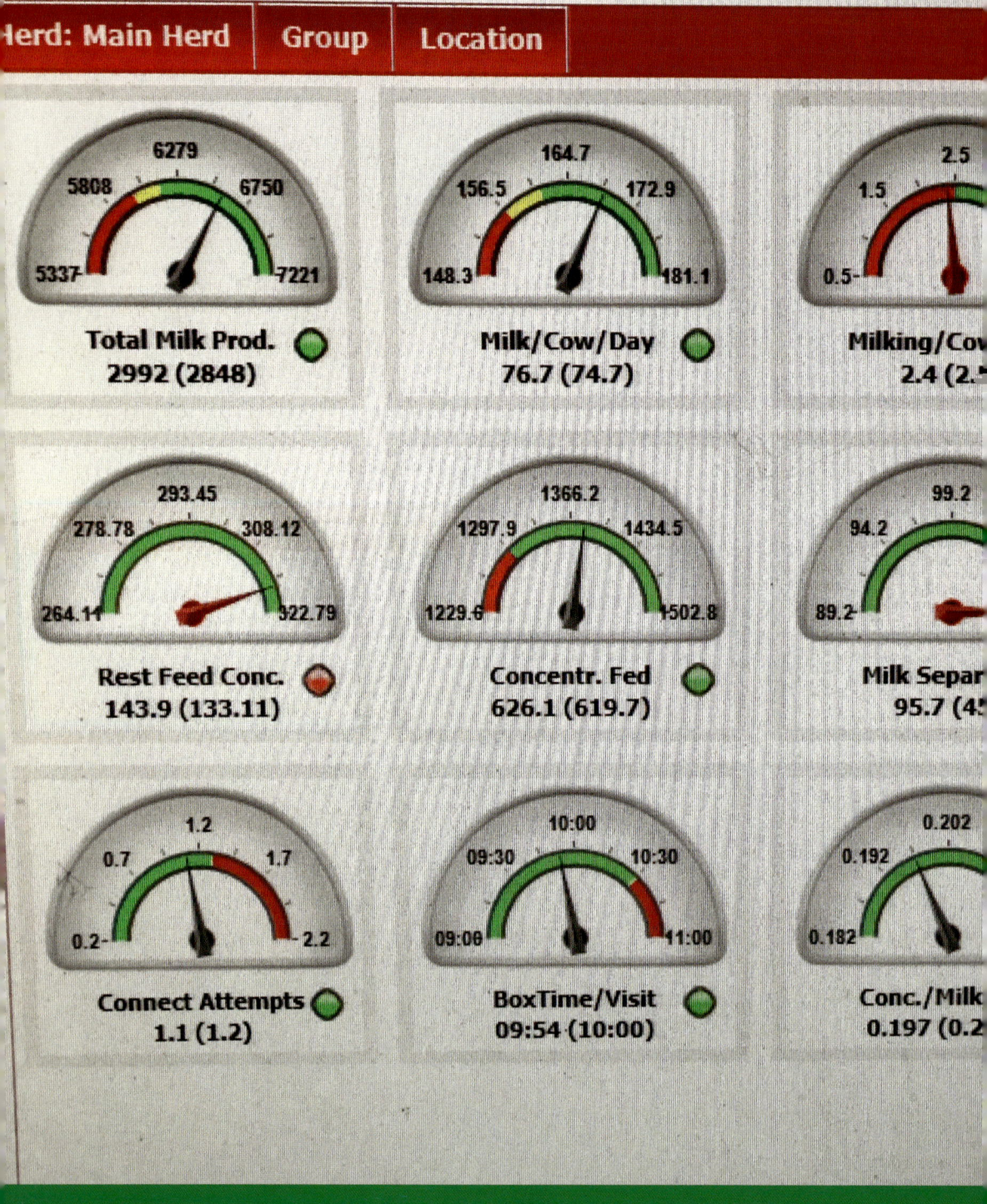

The robotic milker connects to a computer, which offers a snapshot of the cows' health.

The Matthews also need physical capital to manage the farm. Their robotic milker is a key piece of equipment that has the following benefits:

- The farm has limited staff, so the robot reduces physical strain on Sam and Carolyn.
- The milker's cleaning tools such as udder brushes promote good hygiene.
- The cows are milked more frequently, creating better **outputs**.
- The milker measures the amount of milk produced. That determines how much feed is needed. This allows the Matthews to manage food costs.
- Computerized monitoring checks the health of the cows at each milking.
- The time saved from the labor of milking allows for extra care to be given to cows that need it.

After the cows are milked, other machines are needed to make the milk into ice cream. The milk temporarily leaves the farm and heads 27 miles (43 kilometers) north to Longacres Modern Dairy for **homogenization** and processing into an ice cream base mix.

...ody's Mocha Chip	Flora's Lavender & Cream
...spberry Lemonade Sorbet	Milky Way Vanilla
...Tara's Tiramisù	Classic's Rich Coffee
...nne's Rocky Road	Bessie's Black Raspber...
...om's Butter Pecan	Molly's Mint Chocolate C...
...anilla Fudge Ripple	Flossie's Root Beer Fl...
...Razzamatazz Truffle	Duchess's Chocolate Supre...
...neva's Chocolate	Hazel's "Moo"tella
...er's Sweet Strawberry	Claire's Cookies-n-Cre...

Your Favorite Premium H...de Ice Cream: It's Moolicio...

Each flavor at the creamery honors a past or present member of the herd.

Then it is returned to the farm.

When the mix returns to the farm, it is churned into ice cream in a horizontal mixer. Basically, ice cream is milk and sugar that freezes as it's whipped. As the ice cream is whipped,

A World of Resources

The Matthews are agricultural entrepreneurs. This means that they coordinate the resources (or **inputs**) below to make products (or outputs).

Natural Resources—Land: Natural resources are just what they sound like: materials that come directly from nature. These resources exist without human intervention. Some natural resources, like the sun and wind, are **renewable**. Others, like oil and coal, are **nonrenewable**. What natural resources can you identify on Milky Way Farm?

Human Resources—Labor: Human resources are the "people" aspect of the farm. Together, the Matthews and their team have knowledge, skills, experience, and abilities that allow the farm to run.

Physical Resources—Capital: Physical resources are the things you need to help operate a business, like machines, computers, and buildings. What physical resources do the Matthews need to run the farm and creamery?

[Nature's Makers]

The Matthews family makes sure that only the best ingredients go into their ice cream.

24

flavoring is added. It is then packaged into pint- or quart-size containers for take home enjoyment, or into 2.5 gallon (9.5 liter) boxes for scooping in the retail space.

Each flavor of ice cream at Chester Springs Creamery is named after a cow in the herd. Carolyn explains, "There is always a great discussion when we name a flavor. Molly's Mint Chocolate Chip was named after the very first cow on the farm."

Naming is a group decision, involving family and staff. Everyone who works on the farm also plays a part in the taste-testing process—not a bad job if you can get it!

Building Flavors

Milk, sugar, cream, and flavorings, like chocolate or mint, are the key ingredients in ice cream. The milk for Chester Springs Creamery's ice cream comes from the cows on their farm. Other needed ingredients come from other food producers.

Part of the Matthews' job is to carefully select these food items to blend with the milk from their herd. This ensures the best possible product.

Meeting Customer Needs

Chester Springs Creamery serves ice cream from April through November. Customers can enjoy their ice cream at the farm or purchase a pint to enjoy at home.

Carolyn explains that a visit to the farm provides more than just ice cream. "It's a community meeting place—people come, they gather, they hold events here." She continues, "The beauty of ice cream and the farm is that we get people of all ages. We always make sure we have something everyone can enjoy, including sorbets and sugar-free options."

Chester Springs Creamery meets a special need, as a place to connect and reconnect with family and friends.

The ice cream and farm experience at Chester Springs Creamery draws visitors in spring, summer, and fall.

Visitors to the farm get to interact not only with the cows, but also with the other resident animals, like this curious goat.

Each year, more than 5,000 students from five Pennsylvania counties visit the farm. The children get to meet not just the cows, but also pigs, sheep, goats, and hens. These school visitors and summer campers get a real sense of farm life. They learn about what products different animals are used to produce and the resources needed to make them.

The Matthews family believes in educating all visitors about **sustainability** and the value of supporting local farmers. Carolyn, a former teacher, even wrote a kids' book, *The Magic of Milky Way Farm*. This book introduces children to **agribusiness** and dairy farming through the big, brown eyes of a cow named Blossom and her calf, Buttercup.

Maybe someday, you can visit the farm to sample Blossom's Butter Pecan, Cleo's Coconut, or Molly's Mint Chocolate Chip.

Read, Research, Write

Cows and the Climate—Challenges and Solutions

Brace yourselves: this topic *might* not be super glamorous, but it is important.

Because of growing demand for meat and dairy products, there are more cows on the planet than ever before. When these cows pass gas or burp, they release methane into the atmosphere. These cow emissions are a major contributor to global warming.

Is there a way to reduce the effect of cattle on climate?

Interestingly, cow waste might also hold some energy solutions. Manure (or cow poop) can actually be used to generate electricity through biogas recovery systems. Beyond powering homes, this manure can reduce methane and carbon emissions, diminish farm odor, lessen water pollution, and create fertilizer.

While these biogas recovery systems have a lot of positive aspects, they carry a hefty price tag. Government support—found in states like California—is one way to encourage wider use of the technology.

RESEARCH: What are some other agricultural sources of methane and carbon dioxide? How can farmers reduce the amount of methane emitted by cows? What can scientists and governments do? Is there anything you can do as a consumer to address this challenge?

WRITE: Based on your research, write a short explanation of major agricultural causes of climate change. Follow this with an argument about what should be done to minimize their impact.

GLOSSARY

agribusiness (AG-rih-biz-nis) large-scale, commercial agriculture

cooperatives (koh-AH-pur-uh-tivz) businesses owned by all the people who work in it and who share the responsibilities and the profits

distribute (dih-STRIB-yoot) get an item to a consumer, whether through a store, market, or mail order

diversify (dih-VUR-suh-fye) increase the variety of products or offerings

entrepreneurs (ahn-truh-pruh-NURZ) people who coordinate resources (natural resources, human capital, physical capital) to create a product and make a profit

homogenization (huh-mah-juh-nuh-ZAY-shuhn) the process of breaking down fat molecules in milk so they stay together, rather than separate

human capital (HYOO-muhn KAP-ih-tuhl) a person's knowledge and experience, which they can use in operating a business

inputs (IN-puts) factors needed to make a product, such as natural resources, human capital, and physical capital

livestock (LIVE-stahk) farm animals

natural resources (NACH-ur-uhl REE-sors-iz) materials like land and water that occur in nature that can be used for economic gain

nonrenewable (nahn-rih-NOO-uh-buhl) natural resources that can run out, such as oil or coal

outputs (OUT-puts) the amount of goods produced using various inputs in a given period of time

physical capital (FIZ-ih-kuhl KAP-ih-tuhl) resources like machines and equipment that people need to run a business

preservation (prez-ur-VAY-shuhn) protecting a building or area (in this case, farmland) from development

renewable (rih-NOO-uh-buhl) natural resources that never run out, like the sun and wind

retail (REE-tayl) having to do with the sale of goods directly to customers

sustainability (suh-stay-nuh-BIL-ih-tee) doing things in a way that promotes the long-term health of the environment

wholesale (HOLE-sale) the selling of goods in large quantities to retailers like grocery stores, who then sell the goods to consumers

FURTHER READING

Banyard, Antonia, and Paula Ayer. *Eat Up! An Infographic Exploration of Food.* Toronto: Annick Press, 2017.

Mason, Paul. *How Big Is Your Food Footprint?* New York: Marshall Cavendish Benchmark, 2009.

Rebman, Renée C. *Cows.* New York: Marshall Cavendish Benchmark, 2010.

Reeves, Diane Lindsey. *Food & Natural Resources: Exploring Career Pathways.* Ann Arbor, MI: Cherry Lake Publishing, 2017.

Vogel, Julia. *Save the Planet: Local Farms and Sustainable Foods.* Ann Arbor, MI: Cherry Lake Publishing, 2010.

INDEX

agribusiness, 29
agricultural entrepreneurs, 23

biogas, 30

capital, 9, 21, 23
Chester Springs Creamery, 4, 6, 9, 10–17
   customers, 26–29
   how it operates, 18–25
   importance of cows, 18–19
climate, 30
community, 10, 13, 15, 26
cooperatives, 12
cows, 12, 18–25, 28
   and climate, 30
   food, 8, 21, 25
   milking, 20, 21

homogenization, 21
human resources, 9, 23

ice cream, 26
   cones, 7, 24
   flavors, 22, 25
   history, 6–7
   how it's made, 21, 23, 25
   ingredients, 9, 25
   shops, 4, 5

labor, 21, 23
land, 9, 23

Matthews family, 10–15, 23, 26, 29
methane, 30

milk, 9, 19
   prices, 13
   turning it into ice cream, 21, 23, 25
milking, 20, 21
Milky Way Farm, 6, 8, 9, 10–17
   seasonal activities, 17
   visitors, 26–29

natural resources, 9, 18, 23

physical resources, 9, 21, 23

refrigeration, 7

sustainability, 29